50 Winter Christmas Dishes

By: Kelly Johnson

Table of Contents

- Roast Turkey
- Honey-Glazed Ham
- Prime Rib Roast
- Beef Wellington
- Classic Roast Chicken
- Baked Salmon with Dill
- Herb-Stuffed Pork Loin
- Christmas Goose
- Duck à l'Orange
- Cranberry-Glazed Meatballs
- Yorkshire Pudding
- Scalloped Potatoes
- Mashed Potatoes with Garlic Butter
- Roasted Brussels Sprouts with Bacon
- Green Bean Casserole
- Honey-Roasted Carrots
- Butternut Squash Soup
- French Onion Soup
- Chestnut Stuffing

- Cornbread Stuffing
- Classic Gravy
- Cranberry Sauce
- Baked Mac and Cheese
- Roasted Parsnips and Turnips
- Creamed Spinach
- Truffle Mashed Potatoes
- Pecan Pie
- Classic Pumpkin Pie
- Yule Log Cake (Bûche de Noël)
- Gingerbread Cookies
- Sugar Cookies with Royal Icing
- Eggnog Cheesecake
- Sticky Toffee Pudding
- Christmas Pudding
- Fruitcake
- Mince Pies
- Stollen (German Christmas Bread)
- Panettone
- Mulled Wine
- Hot Buttered Rum

- Spiced Apple Cider
- Peppermint Hot Chocolate
- Eggnog
- Chocolate Truffles
- Chocolate-Covered Pretzels
- Cranberry Orange Loaf
- Shortbread Cookies
- Chestnut Roasting on Open Fire
- Christmas Tamales
- Baked Brie with Cranberries

Roast Turkey

(A classic holiday centerpiece with juicy meat and crispy skin)

Ingredients:

- 1 whole turkey (12–14 lbs)
- 1/2 cup butter (softened)
- 2 tbsp olive oil
- 2 tsp salt
- 1 tsp black pepper
- 2 tsp garlic powder
- 1 tbsp fresh rosemary (chopped)
- 1 tbsp fresh thyme (chopped)
- 1 tbsp fresh sage (chopped)
- 1 lemon (halved)
- 1 onion (quartered)
- 4 cups chicken broth

Instructions:

1. **Preheat oven** to **325°F (163°C)**.
2. **Prepare the turkey:** Pat dry, rub with butter, oil, salt, pepper, garlic powder, and herbs.
3. **Stuff cavity** with lemon, onion, and extra herbs.
4. **Roast:** Place in a roasting pan with broth, cover loosely with foil, and roast for **3–4 hours**, basting every 30 minutes.
5. **Crisp the skin:** Remove foil for the last 45 minutes.

6. **Rest before carving** for at least **30 minutes**.

Honey-Glazed Ham

(A sweet and savory glazed ham with caramelized edges)

Ingredients:

- 1 bone-in ham (8–10 lbs)
- 1/2 cup honey
- 1/2 cup brown sugar
- 2 tbsp Dijon mustard
- 1/2 tsp ground cinnamon
- 1/2 tsp ground cloves

Instructions:

1. **Preheat oven** to **325°F (163°C)**.
2. **Score the ham:** Cut shallow crisscross patterns on the surface.
3. **Prepare the glaze:** Mix honey, brown sugar, mustard, cinnamon, and cloves.
4. **Roast:** Bake for **1 hour**, brushing with glaze every **20 minutes**.
5. **Broil for 5 minutes** for extra caramelization.

Prime Rib Roast

(A juicy, tender, and flavorful rib roast)

Ingredients:

- 1 prime rib roast (4–5 lbs)
- 2 tbsp salt
- 2 tbsp black pepper
- 1 tbsp garlic powder
- 1 tbsp fresh rosemary (chopped)
- 1 tbsp olive oil
- 2 cups beef broth

Instructions:

1. **Preheat oven** to **450°F (232°C)**.
2. **Season the roast:** Rub with salt, pepper, garlic powder, rosemary, and olive oil.
3. **Roast at high heat** for **20 minutes**, then reduce to **325°F (163°C)** and continue roasting for **1.5 hours** (or until **medium-rare, 130°F**).
4. **Rest for 20 minutes** before slicing.

Beef Wellington

(A luxurious beef tenderloin wrapped in puff pastry)

Ingredients:

- 1 beef tenderloin (2 lbs)
- 2 tbsp Dijon mustard
- 1/2 lb mushrooms (finely chopped)
- 2 tbsp butter
- 8 slices prosciutto
- 1 sheet puff pastry
- 1 egg (beaten)

Instructions:

1. **Sear the beef** in a pan, then coat with mustard.
2. **Cook mushrooms** in butter until dry, then spread on prosciutto slices.
3. **Wrap the beef** in prosciutto and mushrooms, then in puff pastry.
4. **Brush with egg wash** and bake at **400°F (200°C)** for **25–30 minutes**.
5. **Rest for 10 minutes** before slicing.

Classic Roast Chicken

(A simple, juicy, and flavorful roasted chicken)

Ingredients:

- 1 whole chicken (4–5 lbs)
- 2 tbsp olive oil
- 2 tbsp butter (melted)
- 2 tsp salt
- 1 tsp black pepper
- 1 tbsp garlic powder
- 1 tbsp lemon juice
- 1/2 tsp paprika

Instructions:

1. **Preheat oven** to **425°F (218°C)**.
2. **Rub the chicken** with olive oil, butter, and seasonings.
3. **Roast for 1 hour**, basting halfway.
4. **Rest for 10 minutes** before carving.

Baked Salmon with Dill

(A light, flaky salmon with fresh herbs)

Ingredients:

- 1 salmon fillet (2 lbs)
- 2 tbsp olive oil
- 2 tbsp lemon juice
- 2 tbsp fresh dill (chopped)
- 1 tsp salt
- 1/2 tsp black pepper

Instructions:

1. **Preheat oven** to **375°F (190°C)**.
2. **Season salmon** with oil, lemon, dill, salt, and pepper.
3. **Bake for 15–20 minutes** until flaky.

Herb-Stuffed Pork Loin

(A juicy pork roast filled with flavorful herbs)

Ingredients:

- 1 pork loin (3–4 lbs)
- 2 tbsp olive oil
- 1/2 cup breadcrumbs
- 1 tbsp fresh rosemary (chopped)
- 1 tbsp fresh thyme (chopped)
- 2 cloves garlic (minced)
- 1/2 tsp salt
- 1/2 tsp black pepper

Instructions:

1. **Preheat oven** to **375°F (190°C)**.
2. **Butterfly the pork loin** and spread filling inside.
3. **Roll and tie** with kitchen twine.
4. **Roast for 50–60 minutes** until **145°F (63°C)** inside.
5. **Rest before slicing**.

Christmas Goose

(A festive, rich, and flavorful holiday dish)

Ingredients:

- 1 whole goose (10–12 lbs)
- 2 tbsp salt
- 1 tsp black pepper
- 1 tbsp fresh sage (chopped)
- 1 tbsp fresh thyme (chopped)
- 1 apple (quartered)
- 1 orange (quartered)

Instructions:

1. **Preheat oven** to **375°F (190°C)**.
2. **Score the goose skin** and season with salt, pepper, and herbs.
3. **Stuff the cavity** with apple and orange.
4. **Roast for 2.5–3 hours**, basting every **30 minutes**.

Duck à l'Orange

(A classic French dish with crispy duck and orange sauce)

Ingredients:

- 1 whole duck (5–6 lbs)
- 2 tbsp salt
- 1 tsp black pepper
- 1/2 cup orange juice
- 1/4 cup honey
- 1/4 cup white wine vinegar
- 1 tbsp cornstarch

Instructions:

1. **Preheat oven** to **375°F (190°C)**.
2. **Score the duck skin** and season with salt and pepper.
3. **Roast for 2 hours**, basting every **30 minutes**.
4. **Make the sauce:** Simmer orange juice, honey, vinegar, and cornstarch until thick.
5. **Serve duck with sauce.**

Cranberry-Glazed Meatballs

(Sweet and tangy meatballs for a festive appetizer)

Ingredients:

- 1 lb ground beef
- 1/2 cup breadcrumbs
- 1 egg
- 1/2 tsp salt
- 1/2 tsp black pepper
- 1 cup cranberry sauce
- 1/4 cup honey
- 1 tbsp soy sauce

Instructions:

1. **Preheat oven** to **375°F (190°C)**.
2. **Mix meatball ingredients** and form small meatballs.
3. **Bake for 15 minutes.**
4. **Make the glaze:** Heat cranberry sauce, honey, and soy sauce.
5. **Coat meatballs in glaze** and serve warm.

Yorkshire Pudding

(A classic English side with a crisp exterior and soft, airy inside)

Ingredients:

- 1 cup all-purpose flour
- 1 cup milk
- 3 eggs
- 1/2 tsp salt
- 2 tbsp beef drippings or vegetable oil

Instructions:

1. **Preheat oven** to **425°F (218°C)**.
2. **Mix batter:** Whisk flour, milk, eggs, and salt until smooth. Let rest for 30 minutes.
3. **Heat drippings** in a muffin tin until sizzling.
4. **Pour batter** into hot tins and bake for **20–25 minutes** until puffed and golden.

Scalloped Potatoes

(Creamy, cheesy, and perfectly baked potato slices)

Ingredients:

- 4 large potatoes (thinly sliced)
- 2 cups heavy cream
- 1 cup shredded cheddar cheese
- 2 cloves garlic (minced)
- 1 tsp salt
- 1/2 tsp black pepper
- 1/2 tsp thyme

Instructions:

1. **Preheat oven** to **375°F (190°C)**.
2. **Layer potatoes** in a greased baking dish.
3. **Mix cream, garlic, salt, pepper, and thyme** and pour over potatoes.
4. **Top with cheese** and bake for **45–50 minutes** until golden and bubbly.

Mashed Potatoes with Garlic Butter

(A creamy and flavorful holiday favorite)

Ingredients:

- 4 large russet potatoes (peeled and cubed)
- 4 tbsp butter
- 3 cloves garlic (minced)
- 1/2 cup heavy cream
- 1/2 tsp salt
- 1/4 tsp black pepper

Instructions:

1. **Boil potatoes** until fork-tender, then drain.
2. **Sauté garlic** in butter until fragrant.
3. **Mash potatoes** with garlic butter, cream, salt, and pepper.

Roasted Brussels Sprouts with Bacon

(Crispy, caramelized Brussels sprouts with smoky bacon)

Ingredients:

- 1 lb Brussels sprouts (halved)
- 4 strips bacon (chopped)
- 2 tbsp olive oil
- 1/2 tsp salt
- 1/4 tsp black pepper

Instructions:

1. **Preheat oven** to **400°F (200°C)**.
2. **Toss Brussels sprouts** with oil, salt, and pepper.
3. **Spread on a baking sheet** and sprinkle bacon on top.
4. **Roast for 20–25 minutes** until crispy and caramelized.

Green Bean Casserole

(A classic, creamy side with crispy fried onions)

Ingredients:

- 1 lb fresh green beans (trimmed)
- 1 can cream of mushroom soup
- 1/2 cup milk
- 1 cup crispy fried onions
- 1/2 tsp salt
- 1/4 tsp black pepper

Instructions:

1. **Preheat oven** to **375°F (190°C)**.
2. **Blanch green beans** for 3 minutes, then drain.
3. **Mix soup, milk, salt, and pepper** and combine with green beans.
4. **Top with fried onions** and bake for **25 minutes** until bubbly.

Honey-Roasted Carrots

(Sweet and caramelized carrots with a hint of honey)

Ingredients:

- 1 lb carrots (peeled and cut)
- 2 tbsp olive oil
- 2 tbsp honey
- 1/2 tsp salt
- 1/4 tsp black pepper

Instructions:

1. **Preheat oven** to **400°F (200°C)**.
2. **Toss carrots** with oil, honey, salt, and pepper.
3. **Roast for 25 minutes**, stirring halfway.

Butternut Squash Soup

(A creamy and comforting fall soup)

Ingredients:

- 1 butternut squash (peeled and cubed)
- 1 onion (chopped)
- 2 cloves garlic (minced)
- 4 cups vegetable broth
- 1/2 cup heavy cream
- 1/2 tsp salt
- 1/4 tsp black pepper

Instructions:

1. **Sauté onion and garlic** in a pot.
2. **Add squash and broth**, simmer for **20 minutes** until soft.
3. **Blend until smooth** and stir in cream.

French Onion Soup

(A rich, savory soup with caramelized onions and cheesy toast)

Ingredients:

- 4 large onions (sliced)
- 3 tbsp butter
- 4 cups beef broth
- 1/2 cup white wine
- 1 tsp salt
- 1/2 tsp black pepper
- 1/2 baguette (sliced)
- 1 cup shredded Gruyère cheese

Instructions:

1. **Caramelize onions** in butter for 25 minutes.
2. **Add broth, wine, salt, and pepper**, simmer for **15 minutes**.
3. **Ladle soup into bowls**, top with toasted baguette slices and Gruyère cheese.
4. **Broil until cheese melts.**

Chestnut Stuffing

(A rich and nutty stuffing with savory herbs)

Ingredients:

- 1 loaf bread (cubed)
- 1 cup cooked chestnuts (chopped)
- 1 onion (chopped)
- 2 cloves garlic (minced)
- 2 cups chicken broth
- 1 tbsp butter
- 1 tsp salt
- 1/2 tsp black pepper
- 1 tbsp fresh thyme (chopped)

Instructions:

1. **Preheat oven** to **375°F (190°C)**.
2. **Sauté onion and garlic** in butter.
3. **Mix with bread, chestnuts, broth, salt, pepper, and thyme** in a baking dish.
4. **Bake for 30–35 minutes** until golden.

Cornbread Stuffing

(A Southern classic with a buttery, savory flavor)

Ingredients:

- 4 cups cornbread (crumbled)
- 2 cups bread cubes (white or sourdough)
- 1/2 cup butter
- 1 onion (chopped)
- 2 celery stalks (chopped)
- 2 cloves garlic (minced)
- 1 tsp sage
- 1 tsp thyme
- 1/2 tsp salt
- 1/4 tsp black pepper
- 2 cups chicken or vegetable broth
- 2 eggs (beaten)

Instructions:

1. **Preheat oven** to **375°F (190°C)**.
2. **Sauté onion, celery, and garlic** in butter until soft.
3. **Mix cornbread, bread cubes, herbs, and seasonings** in a bowl.
4. **Stir in broth and eggs** until combined.
5. **Bake for 30–35 minutes** until golden brown.

Classic Gravy

(A rich, velvety gravy to pair with everything)

Ingredients:

- 4 tbsp butter
- 4 tbsp all-purpose flour
- 2 cups turkey or chicken broth
- 1/2 tsp salt
- 1/4 tsp black pepper
- 1/2 tsp Worcestershire sauce (optional)

Instructions:

1. **Melt butter** in a saucepan over medium heat.
2. **Whisk in flour** and cook for **1–2 minutes** until golden.
3. **Slowly add broth**, whisking constantly.
4. **Simmer for 5 minutes**, season with salt and pepper.

Cranberry Sauce

(A tart and sweet holiday staple)

Ingredients:

- 12 oz fresh cranberries
- 1 cup sugar
- 1/2 cup orange juice
- 1/2 cup water
- 1/2 tsp cinnamon (optional)

Instructions:

1. **Combine all ingredients** in a saucepan over medium heat.
2. **Simmer for 10–15 minutes** until cranberries burst and sauce thickens.
3. **Cool before serving.**

Baked Mac and Cheese

(Ultra creamy with a crispy, cheesy top)

Ingredients:

- 12 oz elbow macaroni
- 4 tbsp butter
- 4 tbsp flour
- 2 1/2 cups milk
- 2 cups shredded cheddar cheese
- 1 cup shredded gruyère or mozzarella
- 1/2 tsp salt
- 1/4 tsp black pepper
- 1/2 tsp mustard powder (optional)
- 1/2 cup breadcrumbs

Instructions:

1. **Preheat oven** to **375°F (190°C)**.
2. **Cook pasta** until al dente, drain.
3. **Make roux:** Melt butter, whisk in flour, cook for 1 minute.
4. **Slowly add milk**, whisking constantly until smooth.
5. **Stir in cheese** until melted. Add pasta and mix well.
6. **Top with breadcrumbs** and bake for **20 minutes** until golden.

Roasted Parsnips and Turnips

(A sweet and earthy roasted side)

Ingredients:

- 2 parsnips (peeled and chopped)
- 2 turnips (peeled and chopped)
- 2 tbsp olive oil
- 1/2 tsp salt
- 1/4 tsp black pepper
- 1 tsp honey
- 1/2 tsp thyme

Instructions:

1. **Preheat oven** to **400°F (200°C)**.
2. **Toss vegetables** with oil, salt, pepper, honey, and thyme.
3. **Roast for 25–30 minutes**, stirring halfway.

Creamed Spinach

(A decadent, creamy spinach dish)

Ingredients:

- 1 lb fresh spinach
- 2 tbsp butter
- 1/2 onion (chopped)
- 2 cloves garlic (minced)
- 1 cup heavy cream
- 1/2 cup Parmesan cheese
- 1/2 tsp salt
- 1/4 tsp black pepper

Instructions:

1. **Sauté onion and garlic** in butter until soft.
2. **Add spinach**, cook until wilted.
3. **Stir in cream and Parmesan**, simmer until thickened.

Truffle Mashed Potatoes

(Elevate classic mashed potatoes with truffle oil)

Ingredients:

- 4 large russet potatoes (peeled and cubed)
- 4 tbsp butter
- 1/2 cup heavy cream
- 1 tsp truffle oil
- 1/2 tsp salt
- 1/4 tsp black pepper

Instructions:

1. **Boil potatoes** until fork-tender, drain.
2. **Mash with butter, cream, truffle oil, salt, and pepper**.

Pecan Pie

(A sweet, nutty holiday favorite)

Ingredients:

- 1 9-inch pie crust
- 1 cup corn syrup
- 1 cup brown sugar
- 3 eggs
- 1/4 cup butter (melted)
- 1 tsp vanilla extract
- 1 1/2 cups pecans

Instructions:

1. **Preheat oven to 350°F (175°C)**.
2. **Whisk eggs, syrup, sugar, butter, and vanilla.**
3. **Stir in pecans** and pour into crust.
4. **Bake for 50–55 minutes** until set.

Classic Pumpkin Pie

(A spiced, creamy holiday tradition)

Ingredients:

- 1 9-inch pie crust
- 1 can (15 oz) pumpkin purée
- 3/4 cup brown sugar
- 2 eggs
- 1 cup heavy cream
- 1 tsp cinnamon
- 1/2 tsp ginger
- 1/4 tsp nutmeg
- 1/4 tsp salt

Instructions:

1. **Preheat oven to 375°F (190°C).**
2. **Mix all ingredients** and pour into crust.
3. **Bake for 45–50 minutes** until set.

Yule Log Cake (Bûche de Noël)

(A festive chocolate sponge cake rolled with cream)

Ingredients:

- 4 eggs
- 3/4 cup sugar
- 1 tsp vanilla extract
- 1/2 cup flour
- 1/4 cup cocoa powder
- 1/2 tsp baking powder
- 1/4 tsp salt
- 1 cup heavy cream
- 2 tbsp powdered sugar
- 1/2 cup chocolate ganache

Instructions:

1. **Preheat oven to 375°F (190°C)**, line a baking sheet with parchment paper.
2. **Whisk eggs and sugar** until fluffy, then fold in vanilla, flour, cocoa, baking powder, and salt.
3. **Spread batter evenly** and bake for 10–12 minutes.
4. **Roll cake in a towel** while warm and let cool.
5. **Whip cream with powdered sugar**, unroll cake, spread filling, and roll back up.
6. **Coat with chocolate ganache** and decorate.

Gingerbread Cookies

(A classic Christmas favorite with warm spices)

Ingredients:

- 3 1/4 cups all-purpose flour
- 1 tsp baking soda
- 2 tsp ground ginger
- 1 1/2 tsp ground cinnamon
- 1/2 tsp ground cloves
- 1/4 tsp ground nutmeg
- 1/4 tsp salt
- 3/4 cup unsalted butter (softened)
- 1/2 cup brown sugar
- 1 egg
- 1/2 cup molasses
- 1 tsp vanilla extract

Instructions:

1. **Preheat oven** to **350°F (175°C)** and line baking sheets with parchment paper.
2. **Mix dry ingredients**: flour, baking soda, spices, and salt.
3. **Cream butter and sugar**, then add the egg, molasses, and vanilla.
4. Gradually add the dry ingredients, mixing until combined.
5. **Roll dough** on a floured surface to about 1/4-inch thickness and cut into shapes.
6. **Bake for 8-10 minutes** and let cool before decorating.

Sugar Cookies with Royal Icing

(Sweet, buttery cookies decorated with royal icing)

Ingredients:

- 2 3/4 cups all-purpose flour
- 1 tsp baking soda
- 1 tsp baking powder
- 1 cup unsalted butter (softened)
- 1 1/2 cups white sugar
- 1 egg
- 1 tsp vanilla extract
- 1/2 tsp almond extract
- Royal icing (powdered sugar, meringue powder, water)

Instructions:

1. **Preheat oven** to **350°F (175°C)** and line baking sheets with parchment paper.
2. **Cream butter and sugar**, then add egg and extracts.
3. **Combine flour, baking soda, and baking powder**, then gradually add to the wet mixture.
4. **Roll dough** and cut shapes.
5. **Bake for 8-10 minutes**. Once cooled, decorate with royal icing.

Eggnog Cheesecake

(A rich, creamy cheesecake with holiday eggnog flavor)

Ingredients:

- 1 1/2 cups graham cracker crumbs
- 1/4 cup sugar
- 1/2 cup butter (melted)
- 3 8-oz packages cream cheese (softened)
- 1 cup sugar
- 3 large eggs
- 1 cup eggnog
- 1 tsp vanilla extract
- 1 tsp ground nutmeg

Instructions:

1. **Preheat oven to 325°F (163°C)**.
2. **Mix graham cracker crumbs, sugar, and butter**; press into the bottom of a springform pan.
3. **Beat cream cheese and sugar** until smooth, then add eggs one at a time.
4. Add eggnog, vanilla, and nutmeg.
5. **Pour batter into pan** and bake for 50-60 minutes. Let cool before chilling for 4 hours.

Sticky Toffee Pudding

(Soft sponge cake drenched in a rich toffee sauce)

Ingredients:

- 1 cup dates (chopped)
- 1 tsp baking soda
- 1 1/2 cups boiling water
- 1/2 cup unsalted butter
- 3/4 cup brown sugar
- 2 eggs
- 1 1/2 cups all-purpose flour
- 1/2 tsp baking powder
- 1/2 tsp vanilla extract
- Toffee sauce (1/2 cup butter, 1 cup brown sugar, 1/2 cup heavy cream)

Instructions:

1. **Preheat oven** to **350°F (175°C)** and grease a baking dish.
2. **Combine dates and baking soda** with boiling water, set aside.
3. **Cream butter and sugar**, then add eggs and vanilla.
4. **Mix in flour and baking powder**, then fold in date mixture.
5. **Bake for 30-35 minutes.**
6. For the sauce, **combine butter, brown sugar, and cream** in a pan and simmer for 5 minutes.
7. **Pour sauce over the pudding** before serving.

Christmas Pudding

(A traditional rich fruit dessert, often served with brandy butter)

Ingredients:

- 1 1/2 cups mixed dried fruit (raisins, currants, sultanas)
- 1/2 cup chopped dried apricots
- 1/4 cup chopped crystallized ginger
- 1 cup breadcrumbs
- 1 cup suet
- 1/2 cup brown sugar
- 1 tsp mixed spice
- 1 tsp ground cinnamon
- 1/4 tsp salt
- 1/2 cup orange juice
- 1/2 cup dark rum
- 2 large eggs
- 1/2 cup flour

Instructions:

1. **Grease a pudding basin** and line with parchment paper.
2. **Mix all ingredients** in a large bowl.
3. **Pour mixture into basin** and cover with parchment paper.
4. **Steam for 6 hours**, then allow to cool.
5. **Serve with brandy butter**.

Fruitcake

(A moist cake filled with dried fruits and nuts)

Ingredients:

- 1 1/2 cups mixed dried fruit
- 1/2 cup chopped nuts (walnuts, pecans)
- 1/2 cup molasses
- 1/2 cup dark rum
- 1 cup unsalted butter (softened)
- 1 cup brown sugar
- 4 eggs
- 2 1/2 cups flour
- 1 tsp baking powder
- 1/2 tsp cinnamon
- 1/2 tsp nutmeg

Instructions:

1. **Preheat oven** to **300°F (150°C)** and line a cake pan.
2. **Soak dried fruit** in rum for at least 4 hours.
3. **Cream butter and sugar**, then add eggs.
4. **Mix dry ingredients**, then fold in fruit and nuts.
5. **Bake for 1 1/2 to 2 hours**. Let cool and store for a few days before serving.

Mince Pies

(Small, spiced fruit-filled pies)

Ingredients:

- 1 package of pie crusts (or homemade)
- 1 1/2 cups mincemeat (store-bought or homemade)
- 1 egg (for egg wash)

Instructions:

1. **Preheat oven** to **375°F (190°C)**.
2. **Roll out pie crust** and cut into rounds to fit muffin tin.
3. **Fill with mincemeat** and cover with another round of dough.
4. **Brush with egg wash** and bake for 15-20 minutes.

Stollen (German Christmas Bread)

(A fruit-filled bread with a marzipan center)

Ingredients:

- 4 cups all-purpose flour
- 1/2 cup sugar
- 1 tsp salt
- 2 tsp yeast
- 1/2 cup milk
- 1/2 cup butter (melted)
- 2 eggs
- 1/2 cup mixed dried fruit
- 1/2 cup chopped nuts
- 1/4 cup marzipan (optional)
- Powdered sugar for dusting

Instructions:

1. **Mix flour, sugar, salt, and yeast**.
2. **Combine milk, butter, and eggs**, add to dry ingredients.
3. **Knead dough** and let rise for 1 hour.
4. **Add dried fruit, nuts, and marzipan** (if using).
5. **Shape into loaf**, let rise for another hour, then bake at **350°F (175°C)** for 35-40 minutes.
6. **Dust with powdered sugar.**

Panettone

(An Italian sweet bread with candied fruits and raisins)

Ingredients:

- 3 cups all-purpose flour
- 1/2 cup sugar
- 2 tsp yeast
- 1 tsp salt
- 1/2 cup milk
- 1/2 cup butter (softened)
- 3 eggs
- 1 cup candied fruit
- 1/2 cup raisins
- 1 tsp vanilla extract

Instructions:

1. **Mix flour, sugar, yeast, and salt**.
2. **Combine milk, butter, and eggs**; add to dry ingredients and knead.
3. **Add fruit and raisins**.
4. **Let dough rise for 2 hours**, then bake in a tall pan at **350°F (175°C)** for 30-35 minutes.

Mulled Wine

(A warm, spiced wine perfect for winter gatherings)

Ingredients:

- 1 bottle red wine (750 ml)
- 1/4 cup brandy
- 1/4 cup honey or sugar
- 1 orange (sliced)
- 1 apple (sliced)
- 2 cinnamon sticks
- 4 cloves
- 2 star anise
- 1/2 tsp ground nutmeg

Instructions:

1. **Combine all ingredients** in a large pot and heat over medium-low heat.
2. **Simmer for 15-20 minutes**, ensuring not to boil.
3. **Strain and serve warm** in mugs. Garnish with orange slices and cinnamon sticks.

Hot Buttered Rum

(A rich, comforting drink with butter, rum, and spices)

Ingredients:

- 2 oz dark rum
- 1 tbsp unsalted butter
- 1 tbsp brown sugar
- 1/2 tsp ground cinnamon
- 1/4 tsp ground nutmeg
- 1/4 tsp vanilla extract
- Hot water

Instructions:

1. **Melt the butter** with brown sugar, cinnamon, nutmeg, and vanilla in a mug.
2. **Add rum** and stir.
3. **Fill with hot water** and stir again.
4. **Garnish** with a cinnamon stick or a dollop of whipped cream.

Spiced Apple Cider

(A warm, fruity drink with festive spices)

Ingredients:

- 4 cups apple cider
- 1 orange (sliced)
- 2 cinnamon sticks
- 4 whole cloves
- 2 star anise
- 1/4 tsp ground ginger

Instructions:

1. **Combine apple cider, orange slices, and spices** in a pot.
2. **Simmer on low heat** for 20-30 minutes.
3. **Strain and serve** warm. Garnish with an orange slice or cinnamon stick.

Peppermint Hot Chocolate

(A rich, chocolatey drink with a minty twist)

Ingredients:

- 2 cups whole milk
- 1/2 cup heavy cream
- 1/2 cup semisweet chocolate chips
- 1 tsp vanilla extract
- 1/4 tsp peppermint extract
- Whipped cream and crushed peppermint candies (for garnish)

Instructions:

1. **Heat milk and cream** in a saucepan until warm, but not boiling.
2. **Add chocolate chips** and stir until fully melted.
3. **Stir in vanilla and peppermint extracts**.
4. **Serve with whipped cream** and crushed peppermint candies on top.

Eggnog

(A creamy, spiced holiday drink)

Ingredients:

- 4 large eggs
- 1/2 cup sugar
- 2 cups whole milk
- 1 cup heavy cream
- 1/2 tsp ground nutmeg
- 1/2 tsp ground cinnamon
- 1/2 cup bourbon (optional)
- 1/2 tsp vanilla extract

Instructions:

1. **Whisk together eggs and sugar** in a bowl until smooth.
2. **Heat milk and cream** in a saucepan, then temper the egg mixture by slowly adding the hot milk.
3. **Return mixture to the pot** and cook over low heat until thickened.
4. **Stir in spices, bourbon, and vanilla**.
5. **Chill and serve cold**, garnished with nutmeg.

Chocolate Truffles

(A luxurious, melt-in-your-mouth chocolate treat)

Ingredients:

- 8 oz semisweet chocolate (chopped)
- 1/2 cup heavy cream
- 2 tbsp unsalted butter
- 1 tsp vanilla extract
- Cocoa powder (for coating)
- Optional: crushed nuts, sprinkles, or flavored liqueurs

Instructions:

1. **Heat cream and butter** in a saucepan until hot, but not boiling.
2. **Pour over chopped chocolate** and stir until smooth.
3. **Stir in vanilla extract** and let cool to room temperature.
4. **Chill for 1-2 hours**, then roll into small balls.
5. **Coat with cocoa powder**, crushed nuts, or sprinkles.

Chocolate-Covered Pretzels

(A sweet and salty treat for everyone)

Ingredients:

- 1 bag of pretzels (twists or rods)
- 8 oz dark or milk chocolate (chopped)
- 4 oz white chocolate (optional, for drizzling)
- Sprinkles, crushed candy canes, or sea salt for topping

Instructions:

1. **Melt the chocolate** in a heatproof bowl over a double boiler or in the microwave.
2. **Dip each pretzel** into the melted chocolate, coating it halfway or entirely.
3. **Place the coated pretzels** on parchment paper and let them cool for a few minutes.
4. **Drizzle with white chocolate** (if using) and add sprinkles or sea salt on top.
5. **Let them set** in the fridge for 30 minutes to harden. Enjoy!

Cranberry Orange Loaf

(A light, citrusy bread with a hint of tartness from cranberries)

Ingredients:

- 1 1/2 cups all-purpose flour
- 1 tsp baking powder
- 1/2 tsp baking soda
- 1/4 tsp salt
- 1/2 cup sugar
- 1/4 cup orange juice
- Zest of 1 orange
- 1/2 cup buttermilk
- 1/4 cup vegetable oil
- 1 large egg
- 1 cup fresh or dried cranberries

Instructions:

1. **Preheat oven** to 350°F (175°C). Grease a loaf pan or line it with parchment paper.
2. **Whisk together flour, baking powder, baking soda, salt, and sugar** in a large bowl.
3. **In another bowl**, mix orange juice, zest, buttermilk, oil, and egg.
4. **Combine wet and dry ingredients** and fold in cranberries.
5. **Pour the batter into the loaf pan** and bake for 50-60 minutes or until a toothpick comes out clean.
6. **Cool before slicing** and enjoy!

Shortbread Cookies

(A simple, buttery classic)

Ingredients:

- 2 cups all-purpose flour
- 1/2 cup sugar
- 1 cup unsalted butter (softened)
- 1/2 tsp vanilla extract
- Pinch of salt

Instructions:

1. **Preheat oven** to 325°F (165°C).
2. **Cream together butter and sugar** in a bowl until light and fluffy.
3. **Add vanilla extract** and mix well.
4. **Gradually add flour and salt**, mixing until dough forms.
5. **Shape dough into a log** and slice into 1/4-inch thick rounds, or roll out and cut into shapes.
6. **Bake for 12-15 minutes** or until the edges are lightly golden.
7. **Cool on a wire rack** and enjoy!

Chestnuts Roasting on an Open Fire

(The perfect cozy holiday activity)

Ingredients:

- Fresh chestnuts (about 10-15)
- Salt
- Butter (optional)

Instructions:

1. **Preheat your oven to 425°F (220°C).**
2. **Make an X-shaped cut** in the flat side of each chestnut using a sharp knife. This will prevent them from exploding while roasting.
3. **Place the chestnuts** on a baking sheet and roast in the oven for 20-25 minutes, or until the shells begin to peel back.
4. **Remove from the oven** and allow to cool for a few minutes.
5. **Peel the chestnuts** and enjoy with a pinch of salt or a little butter!

Christmas Tamales

(Soft, savory masa wrapped around a filling of your choice)

Ingredients for Masa:

- 3 cups masa harina
- 1 tsp baking powder
- 1 1/2 cups chicken or vegetable broth
- 1 cup vegetable oil or softened butter
- 1 tsp salt

Ingredients for Filling (e.g., Pork or Chicken):

- 2 cups cooked, shredded meat (chicken, pork, or beef)
- 1/2 cup red or green salsa

Instructions:

1. **Mix the masa harina, baking powder, salt, and oil** in a large bowl. Slowly add the broth until you get a dough-like consistency.
2. **Soak the corn husks** in warm water for about 30 minutes.
3. **Spread masa** evenly on each corn husk.
4. **Add a spoonful of filling** to the center and fold the husks.
5. **Steam the tamales** for about 1-1.5 hours or until the masa pulls away from the husk easily.
6. **Serve hot** and enjoy!

Baked Brie with Cranberries

(A simple, indulgent appetizer)

Ingredients:

- 1 wheel of brie cheese
- 1/2 cup fresh cranberries
- 1/4 cup sugar
- 1 tbsp water
- 1/4 cup chopped pecans or walnuts (optional)
- Fresh rosemary (for garnish)
- Crackers or bread for serving

Instructions:

1. **Preheat oven** to 350°F (175°C).
2. **Place brie on a baking dish** and bake for 15-20 minutes, until it's soft and gooey inside.
3. **In a saucepan, cook cranberries, sugar, and water** over medium heat for 5-10 minutes until the cranberries burst and form a sauce.
4. **Top the baked brie** with the cranberry sauce and nuts. Garnish with rosemary.
5. **Serve warm with crackers** or slices of bread.

Chocolate-Covered Pretzels

(A sweet and salty treat for everyone)

Ingredients:

- 1 bag of pretzels (twists or rods)
- 8 oz dark or milk chocolate (chopped)
- 4 oz white chocolate (optional, for drizzling)
- Sprinkles, crushed candy canes, or sea salt for topping

Instructions:

1. **Melt the chocolate** in a heatproof bowl over a double boiler or in the microwave.
2. **Dip each pretzel** into the melted chocolate, coating it halfway or entirely.
3. **Place the coated pretzels** on parchment paper and let them cool for a few minutes.
4. **Drizzle with white chocolate** (if using) and add sprinkles or sea salt on top.
5. **Let them set** in the fridge for 30 minutes to harden. Enjoy!

Cranberry Orange Loaf

(A light, citrusy bread with a hint of tartness from cranberries)

Ingredients:

- 1 1/2 cups all-purpose flour
- 1 tsp baking powder
- 1/2 tsp baking soda
- 1/4 tsp salt
- 1/2 cup sugar
- 1/4 cup orange juice
- Zest of 1 orange
- 1/2 cup buttermilk
- 1/4 cup vegetable oil
- 1 large egg
- 1 cup fresh or dried cranberries

Instructions:

1. **Preheat oven** to 350°F (175°C). Grease a loaf pan or line it with parchment paper.
2. **Whisk together flour, baking powder, baking soda, salt, and sugar** in a large bowl.
3. **In another bowl**, mix orange juice, zest, buttermilk, oil, and egg.
4. **Combine wet and dry ingredients** and fold in cranberries.
5. **Pour the batter into the loaf pan** and bake for 50-60 minutes or until a toothpick comes out clean.
6. **Cool before slicing** and enjoy!

Shortbread Cookies

(A simple, buttery classic)

Ingredients:

- 2 cups all-purpose flour
- 1/2 cup sugar
- 1 cup unsalted butter (softened)
- 1/2 tsp vanilla extract
- Pinch of salt

Instructions:

1. **Preheat oven** to 325°F (165°C).
2. **Cream together butter and sugar** in a bowl until light and fluffy.
3. **Add vanilla extract** and mix well.
4. **Gradually add flour and salt**, mixing until dough forms.
5. **Shape dough into a log** and slice into 1/4-inch thick rounds, or roll out and cut into shapes.
6. **Bake for 12-15 minutes** or until the edges are lightly golden.
7. **Cool on a wire rack** and enjoy!

Chestnuts Roasting on an Open Fire

(The perfect cozy holiday activity)

Ingredients:

- Fresh chestnuts (about 10-15)
- Salt
- Butter (optional)

Instructions:

1. **Preheat your oven to 425°F (220°C).**
2. **Make an X-shaped cut** in the flat side of each chestnut using a sharp knife. This will prevent them from exploding while roasting.
3. **Place the chestnuts** on a baking sheet and roast in the oven for 20-25 minutes, or until the shells begin to peel back.
4. **Remove from the oven** and allow to cool for a few minutes.
5. **Peel the chestnuts** and enjoy with a pinch of salt or a little butter!

Christmas Tamales

(Soft, savory masa wrapped around a filling of your choice)

Ingredients for Masa:

- 3 cups masa harina
- 1 tsp baking powder
- 1 1/2 cups chicken or vegetable broth
- 1 cup vegetable oil or softened butter
- 1 tsp salt

Ingredients for Filling (e.g., Pork or Chicken):

- 2 cups cooked, shredded meat (chicken, pork, or beef)
- 1/2 cup red or green salsa

Instructions:

1. **Mix the masa harina, baking powder, salt, and oil** in a large bowl. Slowly add the broth until you get a dough-like consistency.
2. **Soak the corn husks** in warm water for about 30 minutes.
3. **Spread masa** evenly on each corn husk.
4. **Add a spoonful of filling** to the center and fold the husks.
5. **Steam the tamales** for about 1-1.5 hours or until the masa pulls away from the husk easily.
6. **Serve hot** and enjoy!

Baked Brie with Cranberries

(A simple, indulgent appetizer)

Ingredients:

- 1 wheel of brie cheese
- 1/2 cup fresh cranberries
- 1/4 cup sugar
- 1 tbsp water
- 1/4 cup chopped pecans or walnuts (optional)
- Fresh rosemary (for garnish)
- Crackers or bread for serving

Instructions:

1. **Preheat oven** to 350°F (175°C).
2. **Place brie on a baking dish** and bake for 15-20 minutes, until it's soft and gooey inside.
3. **In a saucepan, cook cranberries, sugar, and water** over medium heat for 5-10 minutes until the cranberries burst and form a sauce.
4. **Top the baked brie** with the cranberry sauce and nuts. Garnish with rosemary.
5. **Serve warm with crackers** or slices of bread.